Original title:
Monstera Dreams

Copyright © 2025 Creative Arts Management OÜ
All rights reserved.

Author: Theodore Sinclair
ISBN HARDBACK: 978-1-80581-720-8
ISBN PAPERBACK: 978-1-80581-247-0
ISBN EBOOK: 978-1-80581-720-8

Whispers of the Colossal Canopy

In the jungle where shadows sway,
Leaves gossip in a leafy ballet.
Lizards take part in a dance so grand,
While squirrels debate with a cheeky hand.

A parrot squawks jokes in crisp green air,
While frogs croak laughs without a care.
Vines twist and twirl with a spark of glee,
As the whole forest laughs along with me.

Tales from the Heart of the Rainforest

In a nook where sunlight plays peek-a-boo,
A family of sloths won't hurry through.
They take their time munching leaves so slow,
While ants march by in a hurry, you know!

Turtles tell tales from the old riverbed,
Recounting adventures while others just shred.
The monkeys swing high, calling down to stay,
And the whole canopy joins in the play.

Nested in Nature's Unfolding

A fern in a flaunt, so lush and proud,
Whispers secrets to the passing cloud.
Beetles march in formation quite neat,
While butterflies twirl to a whimsical beat.

The breeze tickles daisies, who burst into giggles,
As grasshoppers hop, doing silly wiggles.
Nestled snugly in the earth's embrace,
Nature's stage hosts a marvelous space.

The Quietude of Verdant Shadows

Underneath the leafy boughs, so wide,
Critters find comfort, and quirks can't hide.
A snake pulls off a prank with a grin,
While fireflies flicker as the day grows thin.

A chatterbox monkey, a caped crusader,
Plots to outsmart a lazy alligator.
In shadows that dance, laughter fills the air,
In this tangled wonder, we all share a dare.

In the Lush Embrace of Nature

In the jungle where ferns sway,
Laughter echoes through the day.
Leaves like plates, they chat and tease,
Whispering secrets in the breeze.

A plant in shades of green and gold,
Tells wild tales, too funny to hold.
With trunks that twist and roots that play,
They dance as if to say, 'Come stay!'

Veins of Enchantment

In leafy realms where critters fledge,
The vines recite a funny pledge.
'We'll trap the sun in our embrace,
And tickle every passing face!'

Their veins like highways, bold and wide,
Host plants that giggle, full of pride.
They wiggle when the breezes blow,
Inviting all to join the show.

A Dance Among the Serpentine Leaves

Amidst the bends of leafy swirls,
The plants laugh low, as nature twirls.
With roots that shimmy, trunks that sway,
They throw a party every day!

The leaves, they rustle, join the jest,
Encouraging anyone who's stressed.
A dance so lively, chaotic glee,
The plants decree, 'Come, join with me!'

Flora's Midnight Secrets

At midnight's hour, the garden grins,
With flora tales and leafy spins.
Each petal whispers, giggles loud,
In shadows deep, they play unbowed.

The moon shines down on every leaf,
They share their gossips, void of grief.
With roots entwined, they laugh and scheme,
In nature's fold, a joyful dream.

Lush Reveries Beneath the Canopy

Beneath the leaves, a squirrel prances,
A dance of joy, taking its chances.
While birds overhead chirp silly tunes,
Nature's laughter echoes through afternoon.

A chubby frog jumps, a silly splash,
Playing leapfrog with a bushy stash.
With vines that twist, it trips on its toes,
Is it a garden, or a circus show?

Serene Echoes of the Jungle

In a grove where shadows play,
A sloth naps the day away.
Dreams of salads and banana shakes,
When he wakes, he's sure to quakes.

A parrot yells with vibrant zest,
"Wake up, slowpoke! It's time for a quest!"
Sipping dew from a leaf cup,
They giggle as they fill it up.

The Heartbeats of Foliage

A leaf sways, the breeze it teases,
Whispers of gossip blow in breezes.
The party starts at the root's grand hall,
With veggies and bugs mingling, oh what a ball!

The beetles boast of their shiny backs,
While worms sway in colorful tracks.
Every creature pitches in a cheer,
Life's a stomp, let's party here!

A Tapestry of Tranquility

Among the greens, a snake takes a nap,
Too lazy to join in the fun rap.
While ants march in a comical line,
Their tiny feet dance—oh, isn't it fine?

The moon peeks through, a silver sly sprite,
Hanging out till the sun says goodnight.
With creatures frolicking, it's quite the scene,
Who knew the jungle was so serene?

Essence Captured in Forest Hues

In a jungle of green, things begin to sway,
A leaf tosses its head, in a comical way.
It whispers a joke as the sun starts to beam,
Caught in the sunlight, it's living the dream.

Lizards in sunglasses lounge on a leaf,
Chasing the sunlight, their ultimate thief.
A dance of the flora, a party unfolds,
With vines intertwining like stories retold.

A snail on a mission, he's lost in the fray,
Sliding on humor, he's leading the way.
That fern in the corner starts cracking a smile,
Reminding us all to stick around for a while.

In colors so bright, the fun never stops,
A cactus jokes, "I'm just here for the props!"
Every petal and leaf, a giggle they share,
In this forest of mirth, there's joy in the air.

Suspended in Lush Whisperings

Under the canopy where giggles reside,
Fronds dance with laughter, "Come join, take a ride!"
A chameleon yells, "I'm the life of the show!"
With colors that shift, stealing all of the glow.

The breeze tells a story, a comic delight,
As mushrooms plot mischief, all through the night.
A raccoon in boots says, "Let's throw a feast!"
While ferns play the music, the night's fun increased.

Hummingbirds hover, they're buzzing with schemes,
Making nectar cocktails with glittering dreams.
They celebrate life in a flurry of flight,
In this kingdom of laughter, all seem just right.

Leaping from shadows, the critters take turns,
Roasting tall tales by the flickering ferns.
In this leafy montage, it's all but a jest,
Where joy is the secret, and laughter's the quest.

The Allure of Leafy Nostalgia

In the attic of leaves where memories spin,
A plant revels, laughing, "Now where do I begin?"
With vines that remember each story they hold,
In the language of laughter, the past is retold.

A vintage bouquet throws a party so grand,
With pollen confetti, it's a whimsical band.
Petals gossip softly, sharing tales of old,
Where every rustling leaf has joy to unfold.

A wise old sapling, with humor quite spry,
Claims, "Time's like a vine, just watch as it spry!"
Teacups on branches, with laughter they clink,
In this cozy glade, there's no time to think.

Wrapped in nostalgia, the fun never fades,
Nature's own comedy, in leafy parades.
Every snap and every crackle, a giggle ignites,
In this forest of whimsy, we dance through the nights.

Echoing Petals in Moonlight

In the garden, shadows dance,
A lizard twirls in leaf romance.
The moonlight giggles, soft and bright,
While flowers plot to steal the night.

Stars may wink, but plants conspire,
To grow a joke on garden wire.
The vines are tangled in a twist,
As petals shout, "You can't resist!"

The breeze joins in, a playful muse,
Tickling blooms, they laugh and cruise.
In every bloom, a secret hum,
'What next, my friend, let's beat the drum!'

So if you wander past this scene,
Beware of plants that might turn mean!
With leafy fans and roots galore,
They'll tickle your toes, and beg for more!

Dappled Dreams of the Tropics

In bright jungles, light plays tricks,
Lizards hide in leafy bricks.
Coconuts start singing songs,
As parakeets join in along!

Palm fronds wave like goofy folks,
Belly-laughs from hidden croaks.
A monkey swings with style and grace,
While iguanas join the race.

Serenading with a gentle sway,
Plants plot mischief on a sunny day.
A cactus tries a dance, oh dear,
But ends up pricking all too near!

Garden paths are paved with cheer,
Botanical giggles fill the air.
So tiptoe lightly, do not fret,
For tropical dreams bring joy, you bet!

Breath of the Wild Garden

In wild corners of the yard,
Silly daisies stand on guard.
They gossip low, those cheeky buds,
Plotting tricks with bouncing suds.

A tulip's eye winks at a bee,
'Come on over and dance with me!'
But the bees just roll their eyes,
And buzz away with quick replies.

The sunflowers laugh, they rise up tall,
While daisies dare them to take a fall.
With roots entwined in mischief's flow,
The sassy blooms put on a show!

In the wild, joy fills the air,
Laughter twirls without a care.
So plant your dreams, let giggles soar,
In this wild garden, there's always more!

The Enchantment of Leafy Whispers

Amid the greens, a secret scheme,
Leaves chuckle softly, crafting dreams.
They whisper tales of sunny days,
And giggle as the sunlight plays.

A sprout decides to wear a hat,
While worms request a party mat.
The ferns groove to their leafy beat,
In this enchanted garden sweet.

Lettuce joins in just for fun,
Making salads on the run!
Tomatoes blush, "We're kind of shy,"
But shout, "Let's raise a toast! Oh my!"

So wander through this leafy land,
Where plants give life a helping hand.
With laughter shared in every nook,
You'll find your joy in every book!

The Allure of the Dense Green

In a jungle of leaves, oh what a sight,
A gnome made of moss, he dances with fright.
He twirls in the shade, under ferns he does prance,
Waving at shadows, inviting a chance.

The vines whisper secrets, they gossip and jest,
Of critters and fantasies that never let rest.
A monkey in pajamas swings high with a shout,
Sipping on nectar, he burps, then jumps out.

Fantasies Beneath the Ferns

Beneath every fern, a party awaits,
With twinkling long leaves, celebrating mates.
The beetles all cheer, dressed fine in their suits,
While the toads tap their feet in big floppy boots.

A snail with a top hat slides down from his throne,
With a laugh like a trumpet, he claims it his own.
"Let's dance on the leaf, let's groove under more,
With daisies for chairs, and the wind as our chore!"

A Journey Through Green Intimacy

In a land where the leaves weave stories untold,
A cactus in sneakers sings brave and bold.
A tour guide named Fern, with a smile like the sun,
Says, "Follow the rhythms, we'll dance, oh what fun!"

The raindrops like marbles roll down from the sky,
While squirrels in glasses make coffee nearby.
Every turn has a giggle, each corner a cheer,
In this realm where the green whispers secrets we hear.

Sorcery in the Folds of the Green

Oh, the magic that lives in the folds of the green,
Where fairies in pajamas concoct their cuisine.
With petals as plates and roots made of spice,
They brew up a potion that's oh so nice.

A wizard who's clumsy tries spells on a sprout,
Turns cabbage to candy, oh what's that about?
He trips on a vine, falls flat on his face,
The leaves all go wild, there's laughter in space.

Underneath Vines of Reverie

In the jungle of my mind, I trip,
Where vines whisper secrets, and raccoons slip.
A dance of leaves, a giggle here,
A parrot laughs while sipping beer.

Lurking shadows in a leafy flair,
I swear I saw a squirrel with hair!
He juggles acorns, makes me grin,
Beneath the greens, let chaos begin.

Spinning webs of dreams so bright,
The cacophony of day and night.
A lizard dons a tiny hat,
While frogs gossip - fancy that!

When the sun dips low, the fun ignites,
In dappled light, the mischief bites.
Embrace the vines, let worries shun,
In my jungle, laughter's never done.

A Garden of Evocative Shadows

In a garden where the shadows play,
Plants converse in their own way.
A flower winks with a cheeky grin,
While clumsy ants start a conga spin.

Mysterious blooms hide secrets well,
Whispers of laughter, oh can you tell?
A gnome with shades sips herbal tea,
While mushrooms giggle, just let them be.

The moonlight sprinkles, a party vibe,
As fireflies dance, they take a jibe.
A flower pot shakes, it's quite the scene,
How silly can these greens have been?

Jovial greens under starlit nights,
Each corner twinkles, pure delight.
So take a stroll through this quirky plot,
In a garden of fun, forget-me-not!

Leafy Chronicles of the Night

When night falls, leaves begin to chat,
About the life of a stray cat.
A cricket's tune, a chorus sweet,
Two ferns gossip, with leafy feet.

A trickster vine pulls a prank or two,
As night creatures giggle, forming a crew.
The owl hoots jokes from his cozy nook,
While squirrels spread tales with a sly look.

Moonbeams twinkle on branches high,
As mischievous shadows start to fly.
A plant once snored, now it teeters,
In leafy dreams, everyone's eaters!

So listen close, to rustles and sighs,
In leafy realms where the humor lies.
Nature's canvas, a curious plight,
In nightly escapades, giggles ignite!

Elysium in the Ferns

In a realm where ferns sway with bliss,
They plot and scheme, a leafy kiss.
A butterfly winks, with a snap of wings,
Scoffing at all the foolish things.

Caterpillars orate like they own the scene,
While daisies giggle—it's quite routine.
The friendly snail takes frequent breaks,
Dreaming of racing, for goodness' sakes!

Underneath the leafy, dappled glow,
A party forms; who's in the know?
A hedgehog awaits his royal feast,
With cupcakes made by a cheerful beast.

So come my friend, join the fun,
Under the ferns, where laughter's spun.
In this paradise where giggles gleam,
A serene joy wrapped in leafed dream.

An Invitation to Nature's Dreamscape

Come join the plants in their wild chase,
They dream of fish in a leafy place.
With vines that dance and leaves that giggle,
In this jungle, reality's quite the wiggle.

Around the corner, a cactus does sway,
Telling jokes in the sun's warm ray.
A parrot pops in, wearing a hat,
Chirping out jokes that make hearts pat.

In the shade, a sloth's dragging slow,
Mimicking turtles—they're putting on a show.
Laughter echoing through the ferns,
Nature's secrets are here for the turns.

So grab your hat and join the spree,
Nature's nonsense, come laugh with me!
Where laughter grows and silliness reigns,
In this dreamscape, nobody complains.

Flora's Forgotten Melodies

In the garden, a songbird hums,
While daffodils wiggle, shaking their bums.
The daisies clap with petals so bright,
Throwing a giggle in the moonlight.

A wobbly tree begins to sway,
Dropping acorns like confetti play.
While worms compose symphonies sweet,
With each wriggle, they dance on their feet.

Old vines strum the nighttime air,
As crickets join in, a lively affair.
Forget about silence; let laughter take flight,
To the tunes of the flora, we'll party all night.

The roses blush while the marigolds cheer,
Each note a delight that draws everyone near.
So hum along with this leafy brigade,
In the melodies where memories are made.

The Green Veil of Twilight

When the sun dips low and the shadows grow,
Frogs croak tunes like a nature show.
The leaves whisper secrets to all that pass,
A squirrel in shades, with a touch of sass.

Mossy carpets cradle tiny feet,
While mushrooms giggle, oh so discreet.
The twilight blooms with a silvery glow,
Where nature's mischief puts on a show.

Raccoons laugh over stolen snacks,
While sleepy owls keep the nighttime tracks.
With fireflies blinking their disco lights,
Nighttime frolics reach comical heights.

So wrap yourself in this green embrace,
Where each twist and turn holds a fun-filled space.
Under the veil of this whimsical night,
Laughter and dreams blend just right.

Reveries in a Leafy Realm

In a realm where the wild things sing,
A snappy fern turns to do its fling.
With a bounce in its green little toes,
It leads the parade where laughter flows.

Creeping vines play peek-a-boo,
While a lazy lizard catches a view.
The daisies and dandelions compete,
Who can crack jokes and dance to the beat?

Oh, look at that snail in a funny hat,
Waving hello, think he's so fat!
But he carries the secret map to fun,
In the leafy realm, all worries come undone.

So come take a whirl in this green delight,
With giggles and gags, we'll party all night.
In the whispers of leaves and the call of the bee,
We'll find joy in the oddity, just you and me.

Dance of the Leafy Spirits

In the jungle, leaves do jig,
A party for the tiny fig.
Bouncing shadows, playful sprites,
Twirl and swirl on leafy nights.

Raccoons join this leafy rave,
With their masks, they're oh so brave.
Twirling ferns and dancin' vines,
Giggling under moonlit pines.

Laughter echoes in the air,
Beetles buzzing everywhere.
Dancing roots with mighty grace,
Nature's fun, a wild embrace.

So let's join this leafy crew,
Who knew plants could jig and groove?
In the garden, joy ignites,
As leafy spirits take their flights.

Enchanted by Verdant Vistas

Oh, what sights this greenery shows,
Dancing leaves and toe-tapping toes.
A chubby frog with a top hat dons,
Sings to insects 'til the dawns.

Caterpillars crowd the stage,
In pajama pants, they engage.
A concert held on a leafy roof,
With crickets playing to the hoof.

Vines swing low in swinging glee,
"Join the fun!" they call to me.
As squirrels throw acorns like confetti,
I'm convinced this party's ready!

Bamboo sways, a drummer's stick,
While blossoms giggle, oh so quick.
In verdant realms where fun exists,
Nature's joy, none can resist.

Flight of the Green Butterfly

A butterfly with patterned flair,
Wears polka dots, a stylish wear.
It flutters round like a tiny kite,
Dancing in the morning light.

Chasing shadows, buzzing loud,
With daisies forming quite a crowd.
"Catch me if you can!" it sings,
An aerial show with secret flings.

But owls laugh, "You can't outrun,
A sleepy world when day is done."
With dreamy wings, the games unfold,
Hearts take flight as stories told.

In the garden's gentle glow,
Wings like laughter, sweet and slow.
So if you spot that vivid gleam,
Join the fun in nature's dream.

Tides of Whispering Leaves

Leaves rustle, secrets flow,
Whispers from the trees below.
They giggle, gossip, twirl, and sway,
Turning night into a play.

A breeze arrives, a cheeky guest,
Makes every branch a lively fest.
With every gust they laugh and spin,
In this leafy world, we jump right in.

A squirrel does a wiggly dance,
While pine cones cheer, "Give it a chance!"
The stars above begin to wink,
As leaves conspire, and mischief stinks.

So join the tides beneath the moon,
Where leaves laugh loud, a playful tune.
In nature's arms, we'll sway and tease,
Living life with giggles and leaves.

Starlit Canopy and Forgotten Tales

Under stars, the plants confide,
They giggle low, with roots wide.
A cactus jokes, a fern replies,
In leafy laughs, their humor flies.

One night, a vine slipped on dew,
It wrestled hard, then up it flew.
With every leaf, its grin adorned,
In moonlit shenanigans, they were born.

The trees stood tall, but laughed so loud,
As critters danced beneath the shroud.
Mosses blushed, a comedy tale,
In the garden, life wouldn't fail.

Oh, the stories those plants could spin,
Of muddy mischief and playful grin.
With every rustle, a joke unfurled,
In a starlit world, their joy was swirled.

A Symphony of Leafy Whispers

The leaves converse, a cheeky band,
In whispered tones, they take a stand.
A symphony of rustling fun,
Making music 'til the day is done.

A sloth sat low, its pace so slow,
While chattering blooms put on a show.
Twirling leaves, a delicate dance,
Nature's pranks in a leafy trance.

Each petal knows a joke or two,
Betting on who can make it through.
With all the laughter, sunlit grace,
A playful world in this leafy space.

As dusk descends, the giggles grow,
In leafy laughter, spirits flow.
Chorusing tunes of the verdant maze,
In nature's theater, it's all a blaze.

Beneath the Great Green Fronds

Beneath the fronds, a party brewed,
While creatures danced, they never subdued.
An ant did cartwheels, a snail made art,
Creating chaos, oh what a start!

Vines tangled up, a jumble of glee,
One leaf hiccuped, another yelled 'Whee!'
Bugs were buzzing in hysterical fits,
Nature's circus played out with wit.

Laughter echoed, bright as the sun,
Greenery's whispers, they just begun.
Each petal chuckled, the laughter spread,
While frogs crowned the funniest head.

With shadows long and moonbeams spry,
The leafy friends embraced the sky.
In a night where folly took its claim,
Beneath the fronds, nothing was the same.

Tropical Meditations of the Soul

In tranquil groves, a misplaced laugh,
As palms exchanged their silly half.
A coconut cracked a clever pun,
While swaying gently in the sun.

The pelicans, with pomposity grand,
Waddled about, creating a band.
With every flap, a joke unleashed,
In splashes of joy, their mirth increased.

A parrot perched with tales to tell,
Of a banana who fell and fell.
In vibrant hues, the chatter spun,
Each moment captured — all in fun.

There's wisdom in the whimsy here,
Lost in laughter, drift without fear.
In tropical jungles, where spirits soar,
Meditative silliness, forevermore.

Harmony in the Green

In leaves so bright, I dance and sway,
A jungle party, come what may!
The vines all giggle, twist, and twine,
While lizards join, a grand design.

Oh, the ferns, they wear their best,
An outfit choice, quite the jest!
With every rustle, laughter grows,
Nature's jesters, in leafy clothes.

The critters chirp a silly tune,
Beneath the sun and silver moon.
Together, here, a joyful throng,
In this green realm, we all belong!

So let the laughter fill the air,
The leafy friends, they really care.
In harmony, we leap and glide,
A playful waltz, through green we glide!

Lost in the Forest of Dreams

In a forest where the tall trees grin,
I lost my way from where I've been.
The squirrels laugh with a cheeky wink,
As mushrooms chat and slyly blink.

Each shadow hides a laughing sprite,
Who dances in the moonbeam light.
With branches bending low to tease,
Oh, what a sight! A leafy sneeze!

I follow trails of sparkling dew,
While owls hoot, "Hey, who are you?"
The roots are tangled in a game,
I trip and fall, but who's to blame?

The whispers tell me to stay awhile,
In this quirky wood, each tree a smile.
Together, here, we'll plant a dream,
In this forest, all is a team!

Reflections in the Foliage

In the mirror of a leafy chair,
I catch a glimpse of frizzy hair.
The vines, they giggle, "What's that style?"
As I adjust it with a smile.

The leaves are chatty, full of flair,
With crooked smiles, they comb the air.
They twist and turn, in jest and fun,
A foliage show, all just for one!

I ponder thoughts while feeling bold,
As shadows dance, their stories told.
With every leaf, a secret sway,
In nature's mirror, bright and gay.

Embrace the whimsy, join the cheer,
In every corner, laughter near.
With each reflection, we shall beam,
In the foliage, we find our dream!

Tranquil Pulse of the Wilderness

In a wild place where critters roam,
I find my heart, I find my home.
A gentle pulse beneath my feet,
The forest whispers, soft and sweet.

The breezes tease, and flowers bow,
Inviting smiles, come take a vow.
With every rustle in the woods,
Are echoes of forgotten goods.

A playful breeze, a skittering bat,
Trees wear their hats, imagine that!
The shadows chuckle, the sun beams bright,
In this wild dance, all is just right.

Together with the twigs and leaves,
I share a laugh the forest weaves.
Nature's pulse, a joyful hum,
In this wild place, I'm never glum!

The Language of Leaf and Shade

Leaves gossip when the wind blows clear,
Whispers tickle ears, oh so near.
Laughter rustles in the afternoon,
A dance of shadows under the moon.

Green tongues wag in a leafy spree,
Telling secrets of the honey bee.
Chasing sunlight, they twist and bend,
In a comedic show 'til the day's end.

An Elegy for the Verdant Spirits

Oh leafy souls in vibrant cheer,
Why do you hide when humans near?
We want your jokes, your leafy flair,
But all we see is a vacant stare.

Your chlorophyll giggles in the light,
Yet in the shade, you take flight.
We applaud your leafy masquerade,
But we mourn the antics that you've delayed.

Enchanted Strands of Green

In tangled webs where laughter thrives,
Plant parties happen; they're full of jives.
The pot's a stage; the dirt's a floor,
Where ferns and vines always beg for more.

Oh, who does say that roots can't dance?
They wiggle and jiggle; they love to prance.
A symphony of sways in a pot so tight,
Dreams of escape under starlit nights.

The Benevolence of Leafy Oversight

Their leafy hands wave, 'Come have a seat!'
With the promise of shade, it's a leafy treat.
Laughter echoes through the garden wide,
As petals flicker with pride and glide.

In leafy arms, the world's a jest,
Plants become the friends we love best.
Oh, how they bless us with goofy glee,
In their verdant realm, we're forever free.

Flora's Lullaby in Moonlight

When the leaves begin to dance,
They start their sneaky prance,
A lullaby in the moon's embrace,
Whispering secrets in leafy space.

Creatures giggle, shadows play,
Underneath the stars' ballet,
Petals twirl in dreamer's delight,
Nature's jesters in the night.

Little sprites with mischief bright,
Flitting past, oh what a sight!
Each droplet sparkles, winks in glee,
A botanical circus for you and me.

So close your eyes, let laughter flow,
In the garden's midnight show,
Rest your head, let dreams ignite,
In Flora's arms, till morning light.

Shadows of the Enchanted Grove

In the grove where shadows play,
Sapling giggles lead the way,
Beneath the boughs, a curious sprite,
Hides and jumps in pure delight.

Branches sway like dancers fine,
Creating patterns, oh so divine,
Gnarled roots weave a funny tale,
Of woodland tricksters, without fail.

A raccoon juggles acorns sly,
While owls hoot a comical cry,
Nature's jesters perform their arts,
With laughter echoing through our hearts.

As shadows stretch and moonbeams glow,
The enchanted grove puts on a show,
Let joy arise from the earthy band,
In the whimsical heart of this verdant land.

Whispers of the Leafed Conspiracy

Underneath the canopy so grand,
Leaves conspire, hand in hand,
They plot a dance, a leafy spree,
An autumn ballet for all to see.

Mice in bowties strut their stuff,
While crickets hum their tune quite tough,
A snail in shades takes center stage,
In this green arena of laughter and rage.

Petals giggle, petals shake,
Each soft rustle, a giggling quake,
In whispers of greens, a secret song,
Where joyful critters all belong.

Midnight shenanigans take their flight,
In the sly twilight, such pure delight,
Under the stars, laugh till we drop,
In a leafy world that never stops.

The Soul of the Sublime Greens

In a jungle where mischief brews,
Spirits of green share their views,
A parrot tells the funniest jokes,
While sloths trade tales, just for hoax.

Vines entwine in a playful mess,
Wrapping trunks in a leafy dress,
Laughter blooms in wild abundance,
Among the greens, there's no redundancy.

Dancing ferns and giggling roots,
Seek to steal the wandering boots,
Each twist and turn, a path of cheer,
In the sublime greens, we draw near.

So come, join the leafy mirth,
Celebrate the humor of this Earth,
In every blade, a chuckle gleams,
In the soul of the greens, we find our dreams.

Folklore Wrapped in Green

In the jungle, leaves do sway,
A gossip vine comes out to play.
Whispers of the trees, so bright,
Share secrets under the moonlight.

A lizard dressed in fancy shades,
Dances on the leafy parades.
Claims to know the best of songs,
But croaks out all the silly wrongs.

Fables bloom with little bugs,
Tell tales of the leafy hugs.
A butterfly steals the show,
As leaves applaud with a rustle low.

In the shade, a silly frog,
Hops along, a wiggly bog.
Each leaf shivers in delight,
As giggles echo through the night.

A Serenade for the Leafy Ones

Beneath the broad, green canopy,
A band of leaves sings joyfully.
Each strum and pluck brings out a grin,
Nature's jive with flair and spin.

The bird out front puts on a show,
A clumsy tap dance, oh so slow.
While vines loop 'round in jesting flair,
Inviting all to join the air.

Caterpillars strut their stuff,
Claiming that they're oh-so-tough.
But round and round, they spin and twist,
A comedy act that can't be missed!

Underneath the leafy veil,
Laughter spreads like a warm gale.
In this jungle, folks do roam,
Finding joy in every home.

Dreaming in Shades of Green

What dreams may sprout in leafy beds,
Where even laughter spawns new threads.
A little ant dons a top hat,
Strutting as if he's the big cat.

Nighttime steals the stage so bright,
As glowworms twinkle, small yet tight.
Leaves sway with a giggling sound,
While echoing joy all around.

Each breeze a tickle, a whispered jest,
Brought forth by trees who love to pest.
They tease the clouds, so fluffy and white,
A playful tug-of-war in the night.

Just as dawn begins to gleam,
Life's a canvas, a swirly dream.
With all these shenanigans so true,
Who needs a snooze? There's fun to do!

The Anthems of Tropical Solitude

In solitude, the leaves unite,
And throw a party with pure delight.
A coconut plays the bongo drum,
As laughter rises, feeling numb.

Each palm sways with a cheeky grin,
Hosting games where all wear thin.
Vines twist and shout, have a ball,
With each little leaf echoing the call.

A parrot spouts his jokes on cue,
Tickling ferns who laugh anew.
The sun breaks through, a spotlight bright,
Ensuring this show lasts 'til night.

As shadows stretch and giggles fade,
The leafy friends will not evade.
Their antics penned upon the air,
A tale of fun beyond compare.

Resilient Growth in the Shade

In a corner plush with green,
Lurks a giant, serene and keen.
Leaves like fans, they spin and sway,
Whispering secrets of the day.

Twirling roots, they dance and play,
Chasing sunbeams that drift away.
Beneath the canopy, laughter grows,
Where even the shyest leaf knows.

Fuzzy vines with a twist of fate,
Decide to wiggle, never wait.
Through dainty raindrops, they slide and glide,
A comedy show in the plant's pride.

So gather 'round my leafy crowd,
Let's giggle under greens so loud.
In this jovial garden, let's reside,
Where nature's quirks we cannot hide.

A Garden of Hidden Fantasies

In the thickets, dreams take root,
A leafy stage where oddballs hoot.
Strange critters snack on moonlit pies,
While flower fairies flicker their eyes.

Sassy snails wear glitzy hats,
Chatting loudly with plucky rats.
In this patch, all fears are suspended,
With cactus jokes, the night has blended.

Fronds that flutter, tease the breeze,
Whimsical whispers among the trees.
Sunbeams giggle, spreading cheer,
In the garden, there's nothing to fear.

Buried treasures are just a trick,
A dance of light, a flick and quick!
Among the roots, where laughter streams,
Life blooms wildly in silly dreams.

Green Whispers of the Tropics

Oh, the tropics hum a tune,
Swaying leaves beneath the moon.
Chirping crickets join the beat,
While frogs in tuxes strut their feat.

Jungle parties without a care,
With palm fronds flipping through the air.
A parrot jokes, "What's for dinner?"
A slice of sunshine, that's a winner!

Lush green laughter fills the night,
With vines that twist in pure delight.
Every plant a story tells,
Of comical mishaps and magic spells.

So dance among the leafy shades,
Where silliness never fades.
These green whispers, soft and bright,
Breathe life into the tropical night!

Shadows Cast by Leafy Giants

Beneath giants, shadows play,
In a world that's bright and gay.
Leaves like umbrellas scatter light,
Making everything feel just right.

A squirrel chirps in deep debate,
While ladybugs challenge fate.
"Who's brighter?" they giggle in jest,
"Let's race the wind, we're all the best!"

Rooted humor fills the vast,
With memories of every blast.
What's lurking underneath each frond?
A comedy troupe of the wild and beyond!

In this kingdom of trunk and leaf,
Laughter blooms beyond belief.
So tiptoe through with giddy hearts,
For shadows shelter laughter's arts.

Green Horizons of the Mind

In leafy whispers, secrets play,
A tree of tricks, on a sunny day.
With vines that wiggle, and leaves that tease,
Do they giggle softly in the breeze?

Banana peels, they're in on the joke,
Dancing together, the plants provoke.
A jungle of laughter, where shadows prance,
In the green horizon, all plants can dance.

Petals that tickle, petals that sway,
With nature's oddities, on a bright ballet.
They plot their mischief from pots and trays,
Whispering tales of their leafy ways.

The green brigade, they sing and cheer,
Conspiring herbs, their laughter's near.
In the wild of home, they play their game,
Nature's elites, they've got no shame.

Fantasies in Filigree Leaves

Under vines that curl like a jester's hat,
Lies a world where plants get a little fat.
In the land of flora, they wiggle and squirm,
Each leaf a comedian, pulling the worm.

Tickle the roots, make the soil laugh,
Each sprout a prank in a leafy giraffe.
With sunshine giggles, they sway and spin,
A show of nature, where do we begin?

Fluffy fronds are the court jesters,
Whispers of puns, they are true investors.
In the garden's realm, in the light's sweet glow,
Fantasies bloom, and the humor will flow.

Green tendrils tickle, with glee in the air,
Nature's folly, without a care.
With each rustle, they crack a grin,
In the world of leaves, let the fun begin!

The Essence of Nature's Poise

Sassy stems strut, in their leafy gowns,
While shadows giggle, the nature clowns.
In the garden's court, they rule the spree,
With posture and charm, a sight to see.

Purses of soil, whisking away,
They plant their jokes, in a playful display.
Chlorophyll arrogance, they flaunt with pride,
In nature's riddle, they won't hide.

With roots like giggles, they stretch and sway,
Giggling petals, come out to play.
In every crack and leaf that peeks,
Lies the wisdom of charming cheek.

So behold the art of the leafy jest,
In nature's poise, they laugh at the rest.
In the essence of green, laughter aligns,
A kaleidoscope of humor entwines.

Labyrinth of Liquid Greens

In a maze of greens, where giggles meet,
Slithering sprouts in the dance of heat.
With every twist, a new joke to find,
In this labyrinth, the leaves unwind.

Jelly-like petals, wobble and bounce,
Telling tales of an oversized founce.
In the verdant twist, where rivals merge,
Nature's comedy in every surge.

Gushing with laughter, the ivy trails,
Tangled with jokes, as the daylight fails.
In this green wonder, where puns grow wide,
Every corner holds a giggling slide.

Wandering through this leafy delight,
Where roots are the whispers, and stems light the night.
In the labyrinth of greens, take a joyful breath,
Dancing with laughter, the only kind of depth.

Dancers in the Sunlight

In a pot, they swirl and twirl,
Little leaves in sunlight swirl.
They dance with glee, a leafy race,
Twisting, turning, in their place.

With a shimmy and a shake,
Photosynthesizing without a break.
Jubilant greens in joyful loops,
Grooving to the tunes of the birds and the troops.

Laughter echoes in the breeze,
As sunlight tickles leaves with ease.
They jig to the rhythm of warm caress,
Nature's fun, no need for stress.

And when the night gets all too near,
They settle down, but not in fear.
Tomorrow brings another show,
Dancers in sunlight, don't you know?

Echoes of the Leafy Realm

In the jungle, whispers play,
Leaves chatter in a leafy fray.
With every rustle, giggles swell,
Nature's secret tales to tell.

The ferns gossip at their feet,
Cursing the grass for not being sweet.
While cacti snicker from afar,
Too prickly to join the leafy bazaar.

The vines entwine, share a jest,
'Who's the fluffiest?' is their quest.
They hang their worries on a branch,
In the leafy realm, there's always a chance.

But when the breeze starts to hum,
The leafy laughter, oh, it comes!
Echoes of joy from stem to leaf,
Nature's playground, a shared belief!

Serpent Vines and Silent Hues

Slithering vines with playful aims,
Twist in the air, they play their games.
Silent hues of green and gold,
Tales of mischief, daring and bold.

'Wrap me tight!' the old bark cries,
While tangled dancers jest and rise.
Like a contest of who can stretch,
In the sunlight, they soon fetch.

The colors whisper jokes untold,
In shades of emeralds, bright and bold.
A leaf plays hide-and-seek with a bug,
Who's having more fun? It's hard to shrug!

And when the shadows start to creep,
The vines unwind, ready for sleep.
Tomorrow brings another game,
Serpent vines with their playful fame!

Beneath the Jungle's Cover

Underneath canopies so wide,
Where creatures frolic and leaves collide.
A curious plant with a cheeky grin,
Peers down, mischievous from within.

'What's that sound?' the roots do quip,
'A squirrel's gossip or a hippo's slip?'
Laughter bursts through the branches high,
As foliage sways with a twinkling eye.

In this jungle, the humor's rich,
From wriggling worms to the mossy pitch.
Every leaf has a secret tale,
Of silly stunts in a leaf-strewn trail.

So if you wander through the green,
Bring a joke, or you'll be unseen.
For beneath the jungle, heroes gleam,
In every laugh, a leafy dream!

A Symphony of Verdant Hues

In the forest of leaves, a party ensues,
Fronds shake to the beat of the morning dews.
A dance of the plants, a leafy charade,
Where vines tell the tales of a sunlight parade.

The ferns wear their hats, quirky and bright,
While cactus plays tunes in the still of night.
With hiccups of blooms and giggles in air,
The foliage claps in a zany affair.

On mossy green stages, they prance with delight,
A brigade of odd shapes, a curious sight.
In this wild botanical garden of glee,
The flora finds fun, won't you join in the spree?

Under twinkling lights, the shadows engage,
Laughter erupts from the leaves on the stage.
Nature's own symphony, a riotous tune,
In the dreamscape of green, we all sing in June.

The Heart of the Green House

In the heart of the greens, where the giggles abound,
A tale of the clovers is humorously found.
The violets gossip while peeking about,
In whispers of joy, they plant seeds of doubt.

The lilies wear costumes and prance with finesse,
While herbs chant their secrets in playful excess.
Succulents smirk, thinking they're the main act,
But the weeds know the tricks that keep everyone cracked.

In pots of pure chaos and laughter galore,
Foliage friendships bloom, oh, who could ignore?
With roots tangled tight like a well-formed jest,
In this house of plants, we're forever blessed.

So raise up a glass of your most fragrant tea,
To the quirks of the greens—come dance, sing with me!
For in the bright heart of this leafy domain,
Every petal's a punchline, no moment is plain.

Under Canopy Stars

Beneath a vast canopy, mischief takes flight,
The stars wink at leaves in the soft, twinkling night.
Petals like whispers giggle and sway,
As shadows of creatures begin to play.

The moonlight's a spotlight for all on the scene,
Where fungi and ferns host a bash quite obscene.
A bashful old root did a salsa so slick,
The others all laughed—was it magic or trick?

With critters in costumes and marigolds bright,
They feast on the moonbeams, a peculiar sight.
Popcorn of pollen floats through the air,
With laughter that echoes, beyond all compare.

So swing on a vine, join the fun of the night,
Where dreams of the green leave us feeling just right.
Under this canopy, joy spills like cream,
In a whimsical world where we all laugh and dream.

Secrets in the Lushness

In the depths of the garden, secrets abound,
Where leaves tell stories, both merry and round.
The rhubarb shares tales of a pie in the sky,
While spinach confesses it wanted to fly.

The valerian laughs, 'Did you hear what I said?
An ant stole my lunch—what a rogue little head!'
And then with a wiggle, the stems all confess,
That moments of humor are what they love best.

In the shade of the bower, the puns come alive,
With daisies that giggle, they seem to connive.
The comic relief from the garden's own crew,
Brings light to our hearts, with each joke that's true.

As the shadows grow long and the sun starts to fade,
The whispers continue, a grand masquerade.
In the depths of the lush, we all find our glee,
Amongst these green jesters, come laugh and be free.

Secrets in the Leafy Labyrinth

In a jungle of green, I took a wrong turn,
Where vines whispered secrets, and the leaves would yearn.
I tripped on a root, with a thud and a thwack,
And a snickering squirrel chortled, 'Now you're stuck in the pack!'

A parrot named Larry laughed at my plight,
'You're lost in a maze, but it's quite a sight!'
I waved him away, feeling quite like a fool,
As I stumbled through greens, missing the pool.

A lizard zipped past like a flash of bright teal,
'You're swaying in foliage; forget what you feel!'
I pondered my choices, should I dance on a leaf?
Yet all I could do was to ponder my grief.

With branches above and roots below,
I found that this labyrinth was putting on a show.
My friends in the canopy chortled and cheered,
As I get lost in their laughter, quite utterly speared!

Somewhere in the Canopy

Up high in the branches, where the monkeys do swing,
I spotted a pig dressed in feathers—what a strange thing!
He danced with a toucan, quite merry and spry,
While I stood on the ground, just wondering why.

A sloth moved in slow-mo, he'd begun a new trend,
With sunglasses and grass hats, he'd surely offend.
The leaves were all chuckling, they rustled with glee,
At the sight of the sloth's new hipstery spree.

I shouted from below, 'Can I join your parade?'
The pig threw a mango, and the toucan just swayed.
The canopy echoed with vibrant delight,
As I waved from the ground, feeling quite out of sight.

Somewhere in the branches, the laughter will stay,
A pig and some toucans, living merry each day.
I'll stick to my roots, as they dance up above,
And laugh with the leaves, for they've plenty of love.

Green Dreams on a Rainy Night

On a rainy night, I heard a strange clatter,
A frog in a top hat, proclaiming with chatter.
He invited me in, to a ball on a leaf,
Where the guests were all critters, dispensing great relief!

A beetle with swagger had brought his best moves,
While fireflies twinkled, could you believe the grooves?
We all filled the air with humorous jest,
As the rain tapped a rhythm, we all did our best.

With raincoats of petals and shoes made of mud,
We pranced like the droplets, each one a big bud.
A hedgehog choreographed a dance with no shame;
We giggled and danced in the puddles of fame.

So if you hear laughter beneath the rain's song,
Just remember this ball where we all played along.
Green dreams filled the night, with joy all around,
In the magical world where the raindrops were found.

Echoes of Forgotten Rainforests

In a rainforest deep, I once found a cat,
With a crown made of leaves, and a fur coat of tat.
He slinked with such style, like a regal old king,
While parrots debated about which song to sing.

The echoes around us whispered of lore,
Of gnomes with their gardens and lost dinosaur.
I chuckled aloud at the tales they would weave,
While vines swung in rhythm, I hardly believed!

A turtle named Franklin laid quite a wise claim,
That wisdom was found in the silliest names.
The monkeys all nodded, they laughed till they cried,
As the laughter resounded, we threw doubts aside.

Those echoes remind me of whimsy and cheer,
Of moments in laughter that all creatures hold dear.
In the heart of the green, there's a party to find,
With echoes of joy, that forever will bind!

Enigmatic Reflections in Green

A leaf once whispered, 'I'm not too shy,'
It peeked at the sun, like a curious eye.
Its shadows danced with glee on the floor,
Saying, "Catch me if you can, I'm hard to score!"

The vines hung low, like jokers in line,
Twisting and turning, all wild and divine.
They giggled at me, with a flick and a sway,
"Bet you can't catch us before we decay!"

The pot laughed aloud, with a clank and a rattle,
"I've got your secrets, come here for a battle."
The soil chuckled softly, 'twas quite a surprise,
As roots plotted games beneath shady skies.

In this lush little world, humor reigns supreme,
Where ferns tell their tales in a whimsical dream.
With each little breeze and a rustling cheer,
I joined in their laughter, feeling no fear.

Beneath the Canopy's Sorcery

In a land where the leaves all wear tiny hats,
The ferns giggle softly, enticing the cats.
They tumble and twirl in their verdant costumes,
As flowers play music with colorful blooms.

The big leafy giants throw a grand parade,
While trolls in the thickets opt not to invade.
With juggling coconuts high in the air,
The lizards are laughing, they haven't a care!

Under the canopy, all jokes should align,
For bark-spitting laughter is simply divine.
The sunbeams join in, with a twinkle and glare,
Tickling the ferns that are growing with flair.

So come dance with me in this magical place,
Where plants hold the secrets of time and of space.
With a chuckle and grin, let's wander the green,
In a realm of pure joy, where we've both been seen.

The Pulse of Jungle Ferns

In the heart of the jungle, a rhythm takes flight,
With ferns tapping tunes that echo at night.
They sway to the beat, with a jig and a spin,
Saying, "Life is a dance, so come join in!"

The insects are drumming, with sticks made of grass,
A party of giggles, as time seems to pass.
The trees form a band, each branch like a bow,
Creating a symphony, stealing the show.

Moss carpets the floor, like a green shaggy rug,
While shadows play hopscotch, a timid little tug.
The vines wind around, weaving tales of delight,
In this whimsical space, where nothing feels tight.

As laughter erupts from the blooms overhead,
The pulse of the ferns keeps the humor widespread.
With every soft rustle and playful refrain,
They tickle our hearts, time and time again.

Dreams Woven from Verdant Threads

In a dream spun of leaves, the laughter is bright,
Where whispers take shape in the soft, gentle light.
The ferns stitched together, with giggles and grace,
Made hats out of leaves for a whimsical race.

The vines wrote a story, but mixed up the lines,
Of a frog who wore glasses and danced with the pines.
They chuckled in glee at their wild little plot,
As the sun peeked in, measuring giggles by the lot.

Beneath boughs and branches, the critters assembled,
For tales of the fragrant and funny, they trembled.
With each tumble and roll, and a whisper of cheer,
They fashioned new dreams from the green atmosphere.

A brewing of laughter, like tea in a cup,
As the roots and the shoots all combined to erupt.
In the fabric of green, where we let our mind roam,
Are whispers of joy calling all of us home.

Secrets of the Green Abyss

In shadows high, the leaves conspire,
Each blade a tale, a leafy liar.
They whisper words of garden lore,
While snails are plotting to start a war.

The vines entangle, giggles abound,
As frogs recite poetry, loud and profound.
The sunlight tickles the ferns with glee,
A dance of nature, in perfect spree.

With every rustle, a prank is planned,
Squirrels are scheming, keys in hand.
The plants are laughing, or so it seems,
In the wild, we dwell in leafy dreams.

So if you wander through this green maze,
Be warned of laughter in leafy haze.
For among the foliage, joy takes flight,
Beneath the green, our spirits ignite.

Beneath a Canopy of Wonders

Beneath green boughs, secrets hum,
Where tiny sprites tap dance and drum.
A toucan's laugh, a parrot's tease,
In this wild realm, it's all a breeze.

The whispered jokes of ancient trees,
Bring giggles that float upon the breeze.
As lizards bask on sunny stones,
They plot their pranks and imitate tones.

In shadows deep, the creatures plot,
To scare the insects in a funny spot.
A chameleon cracks jokes in disguise,
With every color, a new surprise!

So if you seek a chuckle spree,
Come grab a seat, join the jubilee.
For laughter blooms where the green leaves sway,
In this living jungle, come laugh and play.

Echoes from an Emerald Wilderness

In emerald halls where secrets fly,
Cacti chuckle 'neath the wide blue sky.
The thickest leaves share goofy tales,
Of cats that chase their own long tails.

The shadows giggle with every breeze,
As butterflies tease the honeybees.
"Who stole my nectar?" cries a bee,
While frogs just chuckle, "Look at me!"

A lizard struts with a swaggered grin,
Declaring loudly, "I should win!"
Yet every branch knows it's all in jest,
In this verdant realm, we're all blessed.

So tread softly through this leafy scheme,
Where laughter and foliage dance as a team.
For in each echo, a chuckle is found,
Among the emeralds, joy knows no bound.

Genesis of a Leaf-Touched Soul

In the cradle of greenery, shenanigans bloom,
As sprouts of wit break through the gloom.
Each leaf a canvas, jokes unfurl,
As nature's spirits begin to twirl.

Tickling roots play hide and seek,
While the mushrooms chatter, all so cheek.
A squirrel juggles acorns with flair,
While ladybugs giggle without a care.

Petals whisper puns to passing bees,
As daisies wink in playful tease.
"Watch out!" they shout, "For the wind is sly!"
Catching flowers as they flutter by.

So here we find joy in each green nook,
Where laughter flows like a bubbling brook.
In this playful realm, come lose control,
For we are one with each leaf-touched soul.

www.ingramcontent.com/pod-product-compliance
Lightning Source LLC
Chambersburg PA
CBHW072129070526
44585CB00016B/1591